Black Hands

Sandy Freitas

Copyright © 2021 Sandy Freitas

All rights reserved. No part of this book may be reproduced or transmitted in any form or by any means, electronic or mechanical, including photocopying, recording or by any information storage and retrieval system without permission in writing from the publisher.

Write On Books—Grover Beach, CA
ISBN: 979-8-9850685-0-4
Library of Congress Control Number: 2021922076
Title: *Black Hands*
Author: Sandy Freitas
Digital distribution | 2021
Paperback | 2021

Dedication

Dedicated to my grandchildren:

Denver Freitas
Sierra Freitas
River Freitas

My precious gifts

Every year in late September, Mr. Hull would come with his tractor and long armed crane to shake our walnut trees. I knew what awaited me. It was a nasty, dirty job and I hated it. It left me with black hands.

When the walnuts fell from the trees, many were not quite ripe. They had thick dark skins on them called hulls, and I had to pull them off to get the walnuts out. Even with gloves on, my hands turned black from the oil in the walnuts.

My family pulled together to get the job done. That is just what we did on the farm. Daddy always said, "If you don't work, you don't eat."

Of course, we would eat, but we knew we had to do our part to get the job done before the rain would come and ruin our crop.

Everyone worked, Grandpa, Grandma, Daddy, Momma, my older sister, Janice, and me. Even my "**T**" Mary, my daddy's sister came to help. My little sister, Karen, was also there. Although she was too young to work, she sat near the neatly raked rows of walnuts and watched us work. Our little dog, Patsy, sat close by her side and also watched as we worked. It was so important to get the harvest done before the rain, that Daddy and Momma kept us out of school for several days to help with the work. Even though the work was dirty and stained my hands, we made it fun. We laughed, told stories, and enjoyed being together as a family.

I wore one of Daddy's long-sleeved work-shirts and black cotton gloves. A red bandana covered my mouth and nose to keep me from breathing the dirt. The cotton gloves did protect my hands, but they still got stained. When the school bus came down our road, I was so embarrassed, I ran and hid so no one would see me in my old dirty work clothes.

As we worked, we kept the dry nuts and the green nuts in separate buckets. The dry ones were later put in burlap sacks and stored in the shed. The green nuts were set out in the sun to dry on a wire rack.

When the green walnuts were finally dry, they were placed in sacks with the dry ones. Then Daddy would load the 100-pound sacks in our old Chevy truck and take them to the market in Hanford. That was always an important day!

Daddy would come home from the market and tell us how much money the crop had brought. Some years were good and others were what he called "lean."

    Momma however, was always thankful for the walnut harvest, no matter how much it brought. She would say, "That's our extra money. That's what we will use to buy you girls the things you need, like winter coats."

The worst part of the walnut harvest wasn't the dirty, nasty job itself. It was going back to school, with stained hands. They were **black** for at least a week. And then, I had to make up all the school work I had missed.

All week long, throughout the day, I was asked, "What's wrong with your hands?"

Some kids were mean and made fun of me. I had to explain over and over again why my hands were black. I said that my hands were stained from picking walnuts. I described how I had to pull the hulls from the walnuts and the oil from the hulls had stained my hands. I told them my hands wouldn't stay black and the stains wouldn't rub off on them if our hands touched.

I always got through that difficult week at school and I did get my reward for working hard. Each year I got new clothes, shoes, and a coat. With black hands, I proudly wore my new winter coat to school.

The walnut harvest, once an unpleasant experience, is one I cherish today. The neatly raked rows of walnuts embedded in leaves and dirt are engraved in my mind. Along with them are memories and life lessons I hold in my heart. My black hands that I once hated—are now a treasure.

Glossary

bandana	a large often colorfully patterned handkerchief/cloth used as a clothing accessory (head piece, neck piece)
burlap	a coarse heavy plain-woven fabric used for bagging and wrapping
crane	a machine with a long arm that can be raised or lowered to lift or shake
embarrassed	an uncomfortable feeling; feeling self-conscious or confused
embedded	to surround closely
engraved	to impress deeply as with an engraver
hulls	the outer coverings of fruits or seeds
lean	lacking richness, sufficiency, or productiveness
protected	to cover or shield from exposure, injury, damage, or destruction: guard
rack	a framework or stand on or in which articles are placed
ripe	fully grown and developed: mature (ripe fruit)
ruin	damaged beyond repair
shed	a structure built for shelter or storage: especially: a single-storied building with one or more sides unenclosed
stained	discolor: to color something
treasure	something of great worth or value

Author's Note

It is important for children to know that they are created with destiny in their hearts. They have gifts and talents only they possess and can contribute to the world. It is my desire that **Black Hands** will instill hope in the hearts of those reading or listening to it and inspire them to see the value in themselves and others as they pursue their destinies.

About the Author

Sandy Freitas is a retired teacher. She taught Adult Basic Education and Special Education for the California Department of Corrections and Rehabilitation (California Men's Colony, San Luis Obispo, California) for many years. The work ethic instilled in her as a young girl was exhibited and taught in the classroom. She inspired and taught many illiterate inmates how to read and improve their lives. Some have even gone on to earn their General Education Development Certificates and enroll in college. Freitas earned a Bachelor of Arts Degree (Social Science) and a Multiple Subject Teaching Credential from Chapman University. She later went on to earn a Special Education Teaching Credential and Master's Degree. She lives on the central coast of California, with her husband. She has two adult children and three grandchildren. This is her first children's book.

www.ingramcontent.com/pod-product-compliance
Lightning Source LLC
LaVergne TN
LVHW070536070526
838199LV00075B/6791